Creativity Divinity- Anti-Stress Coloring Book Volume 1

J. L. Roman

It's a fact that humans don't need colors to live. We don't need to see colors and if we had to live seeing only in black and white our lives would go on. The ability to see colors is not a survival skill, it's a pleasure that we all enjoy, even if you had never thought about it.

When we enjoy that pleasure using our creativity it's incredibly better. It's like upgrading that natural pleasure using our natural skill. We don't know about you, but when we think about that, we all here at the Creativity Divinity HQ feel so excited that we could literally cry.

That's why we want to share this passion with as much people as we can. We are confident you will do a spectacular job coloring our arts, especially if you do it differently than we would. And what we want the most is to see your finished work, so please, we beg you to show us your creativity. If you feel happy of your coloring skills, please, post it on Instagram with the hashtag #creativitydivinityvol1 and tag us, @creativity_divinity.

We are eager to see what you will create using your creativity.

Everybody loves the colors of flower petals. Do you feel these petals should be colored with one color for all the petals or with twenty five colors for one single petal?

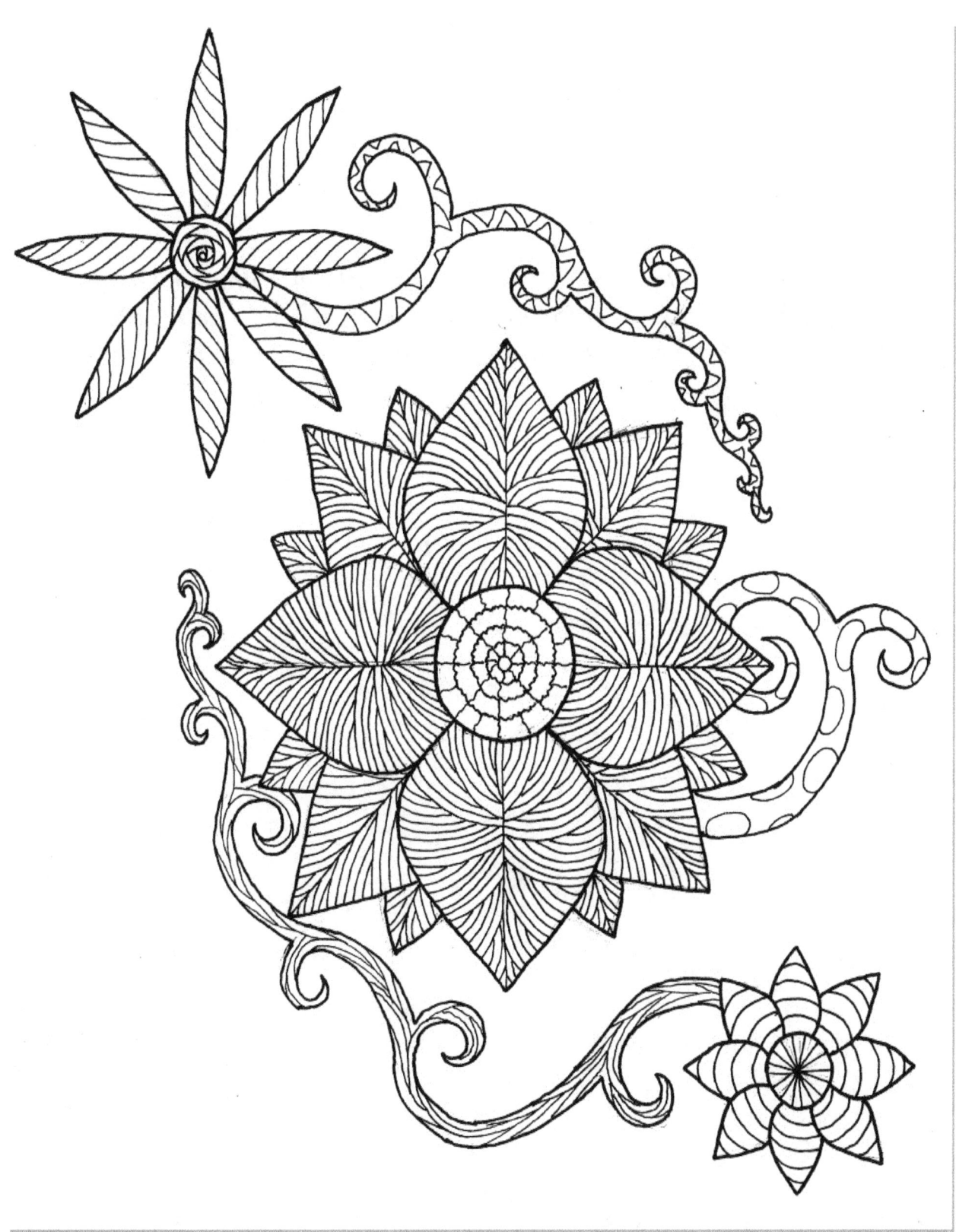

Picture yourself with someone you love drinking coffee or tea. It doesn't have to be someone you love romantically, it could be an old friend or a family member. Can you picture it? If you do, you're ready to color it.

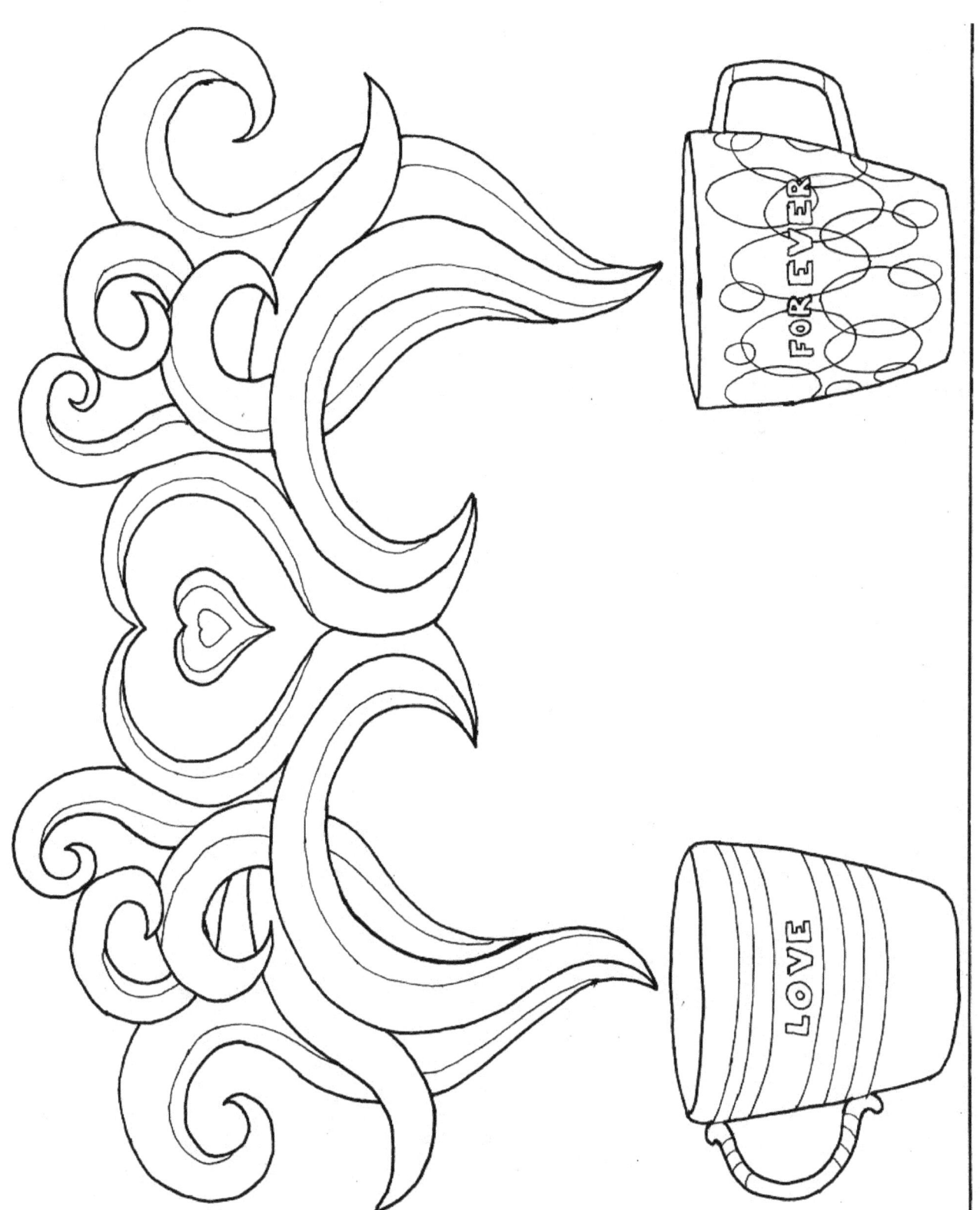

Who hasn't loved a beard in a stage of his or her life? Right? And it doesn't have to be brown or black...

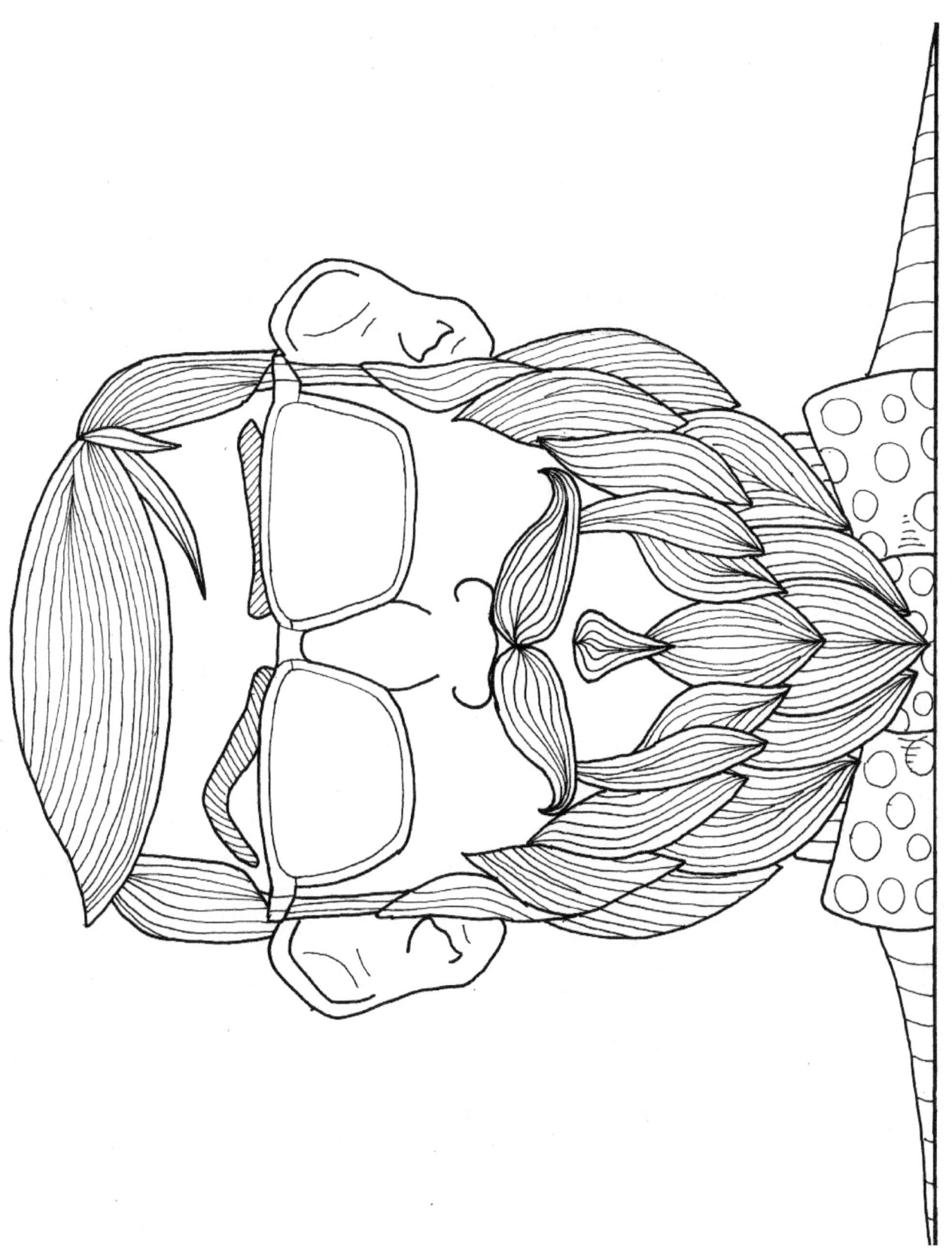

It is a flower, yes. A complex flower to be colored by a complex creativity. Now it's up to you how will you make it look beautiful.

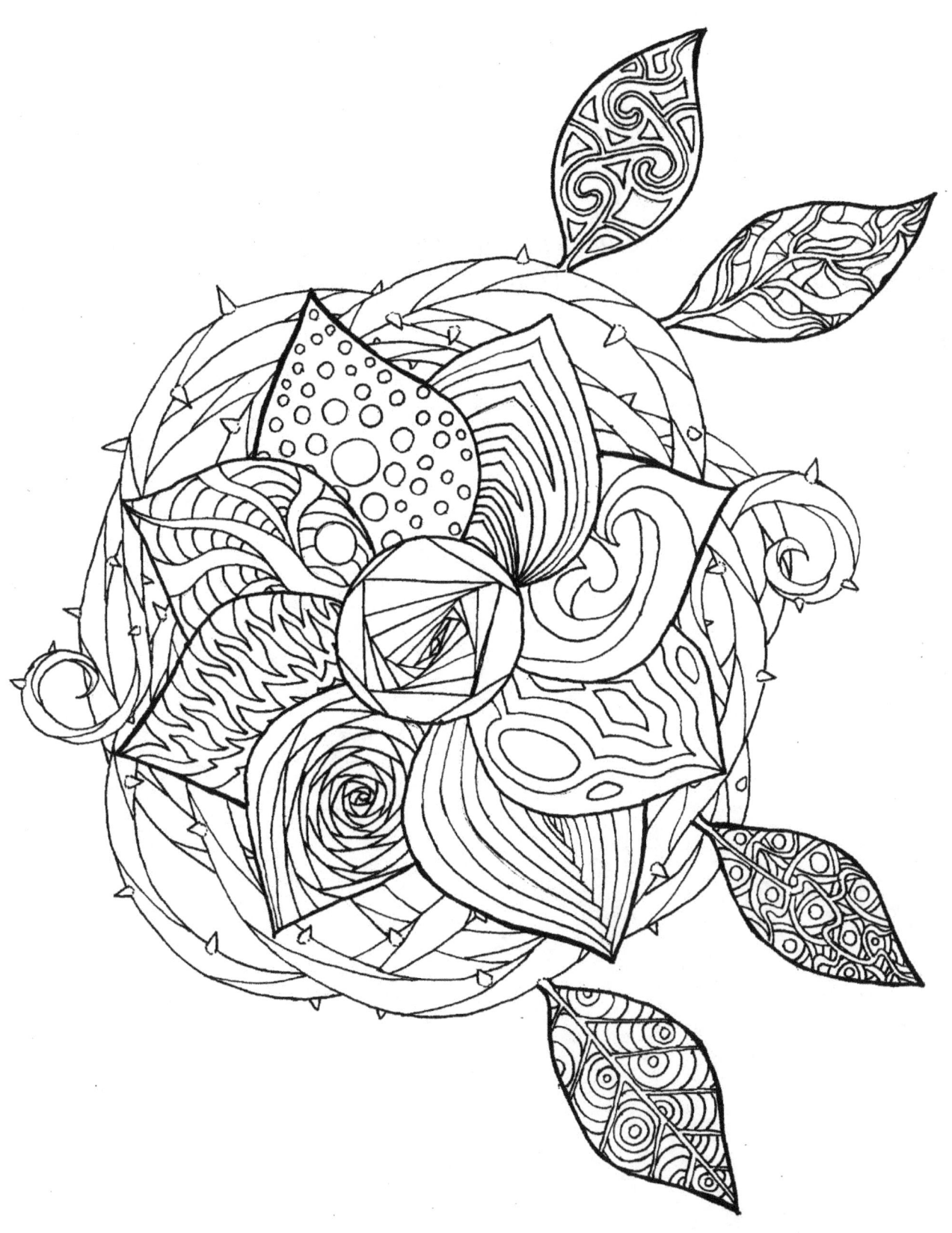

Don't you feel sometimes that flowers watch you? That they have little eyes to spy on you? No? That isn't weird, right?

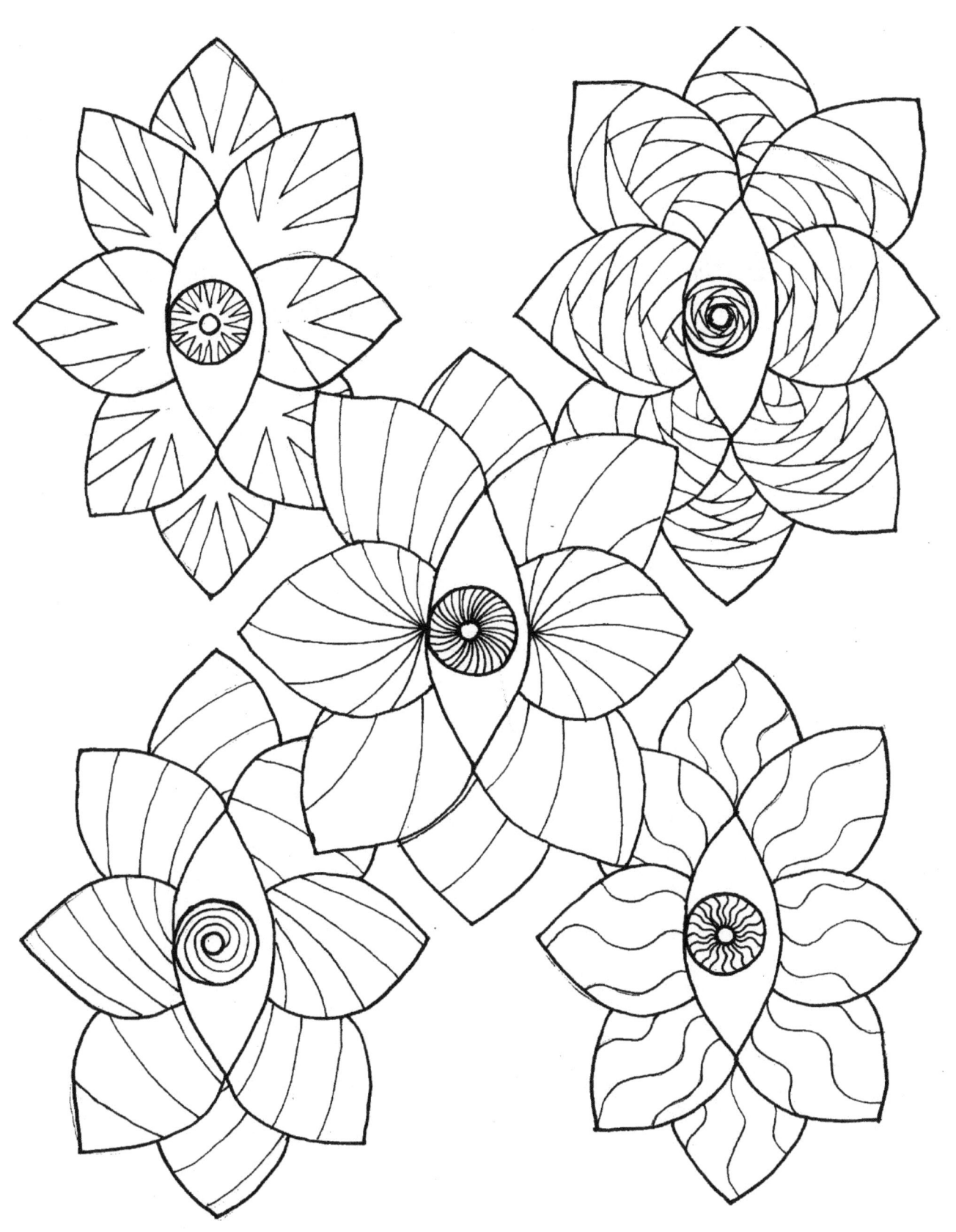

Another crazy thought. Sometimes I compare flowers and birds because of their beauty. How beautiful would be a bird-flower?

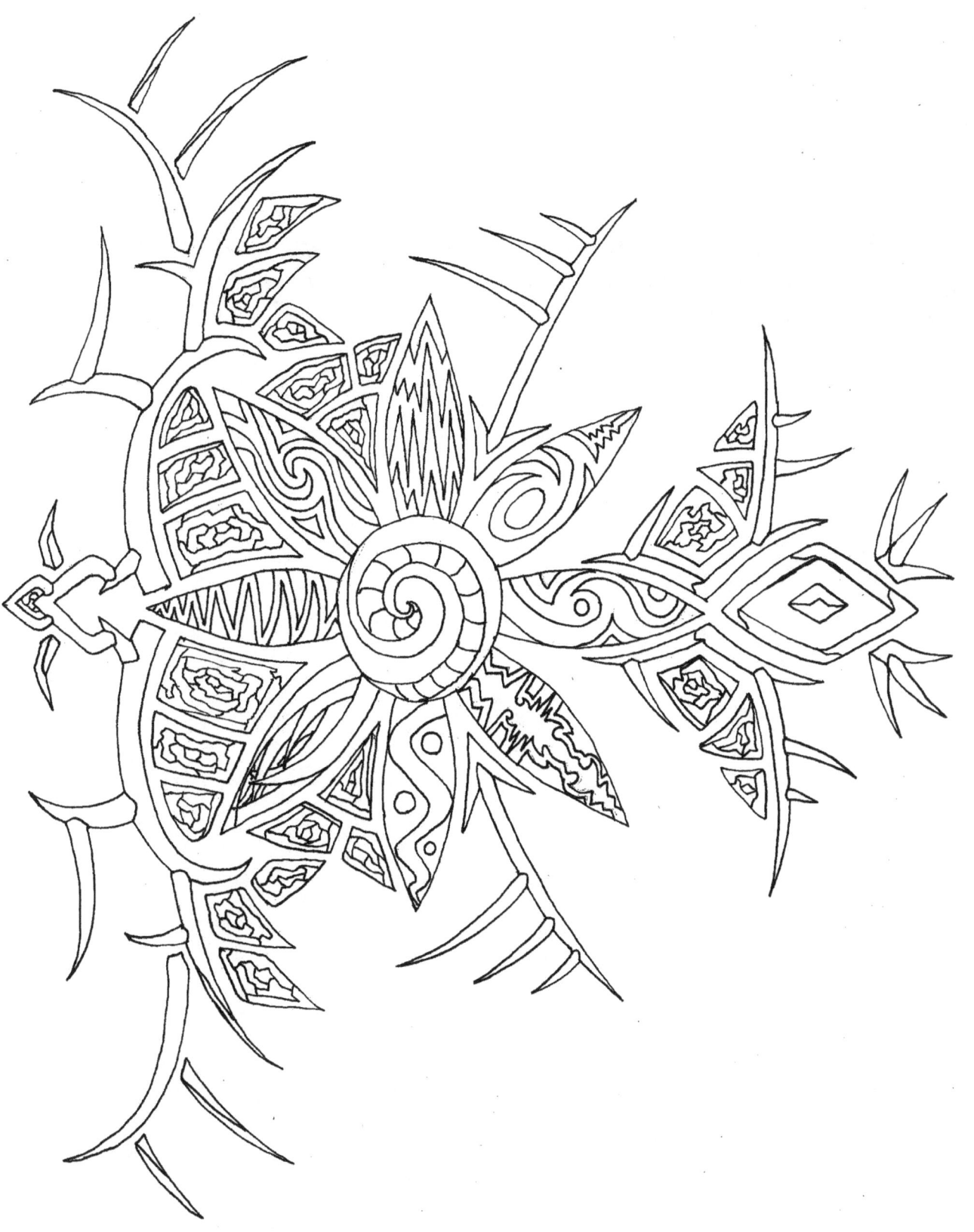

Even in hard times, we all deserve to be happy with our friends and family. And as happy people that we are, we wear whatever color we want and sometimes we paint our faces.

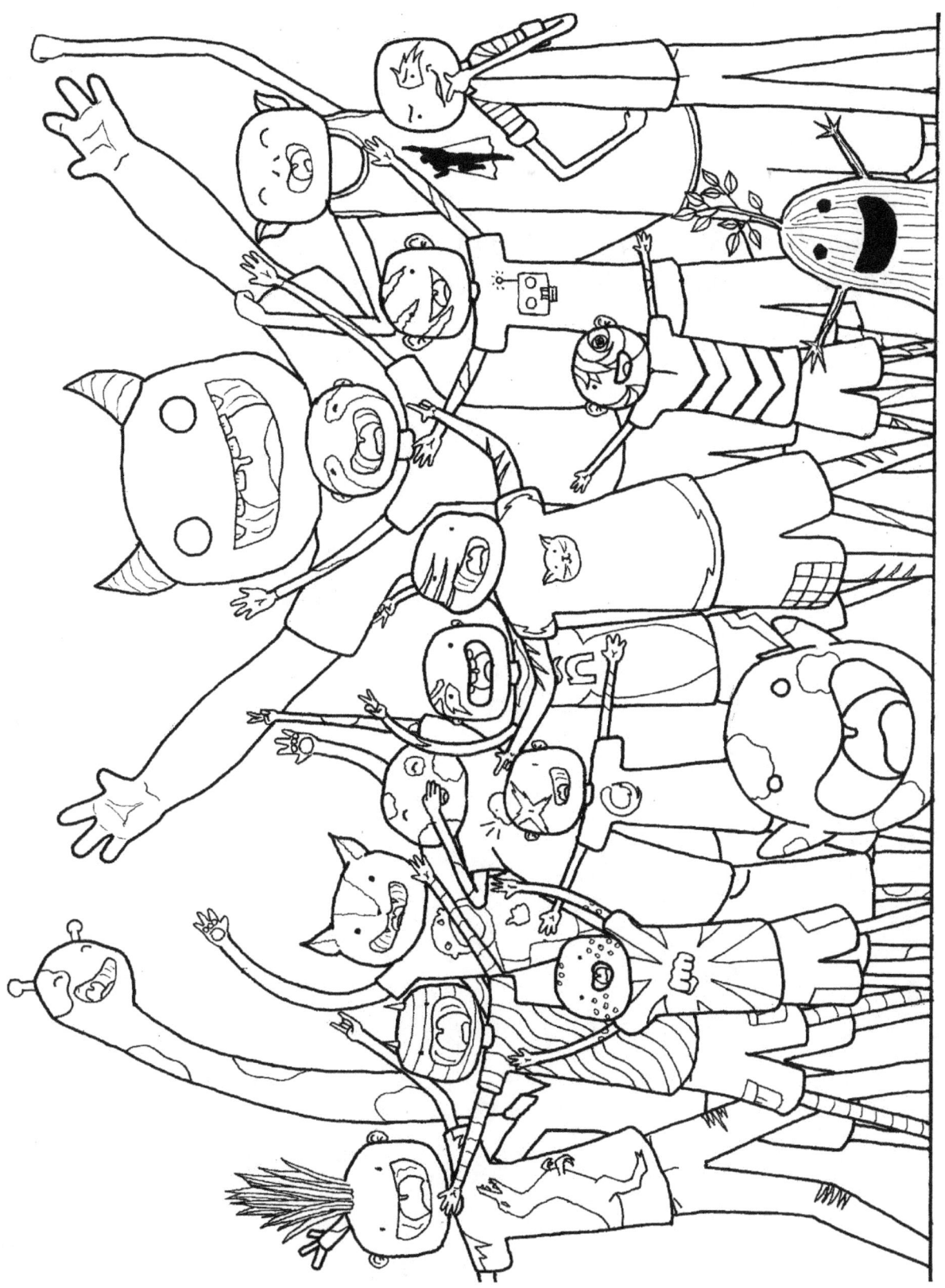

"What's that?" you ask. "Don't you see it's a divine flower that grew on the head of a bald man!? It's obvious!" I answer.

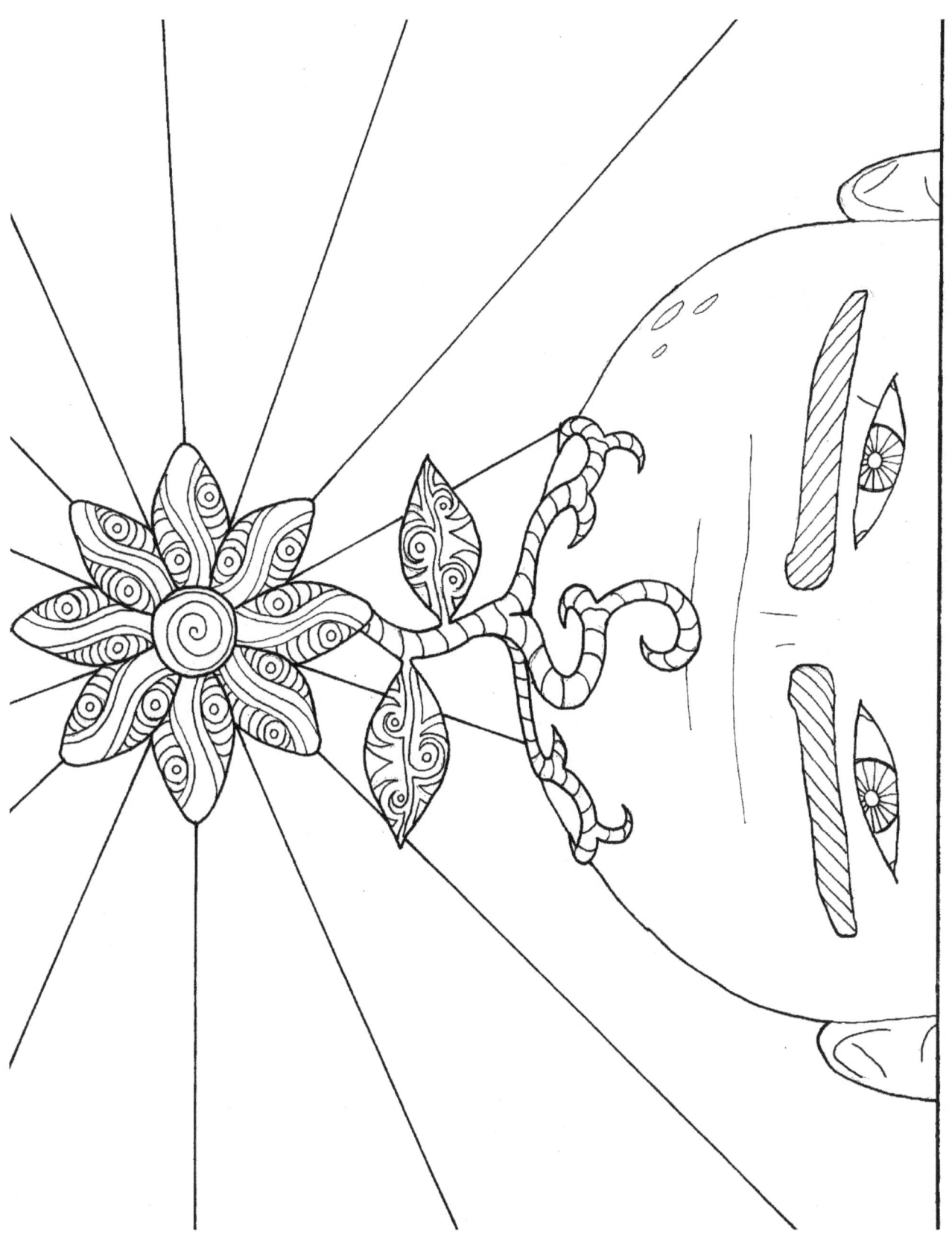

You can't be tire of coloring flowers! Flowers are the best and we can't have enough flowers.

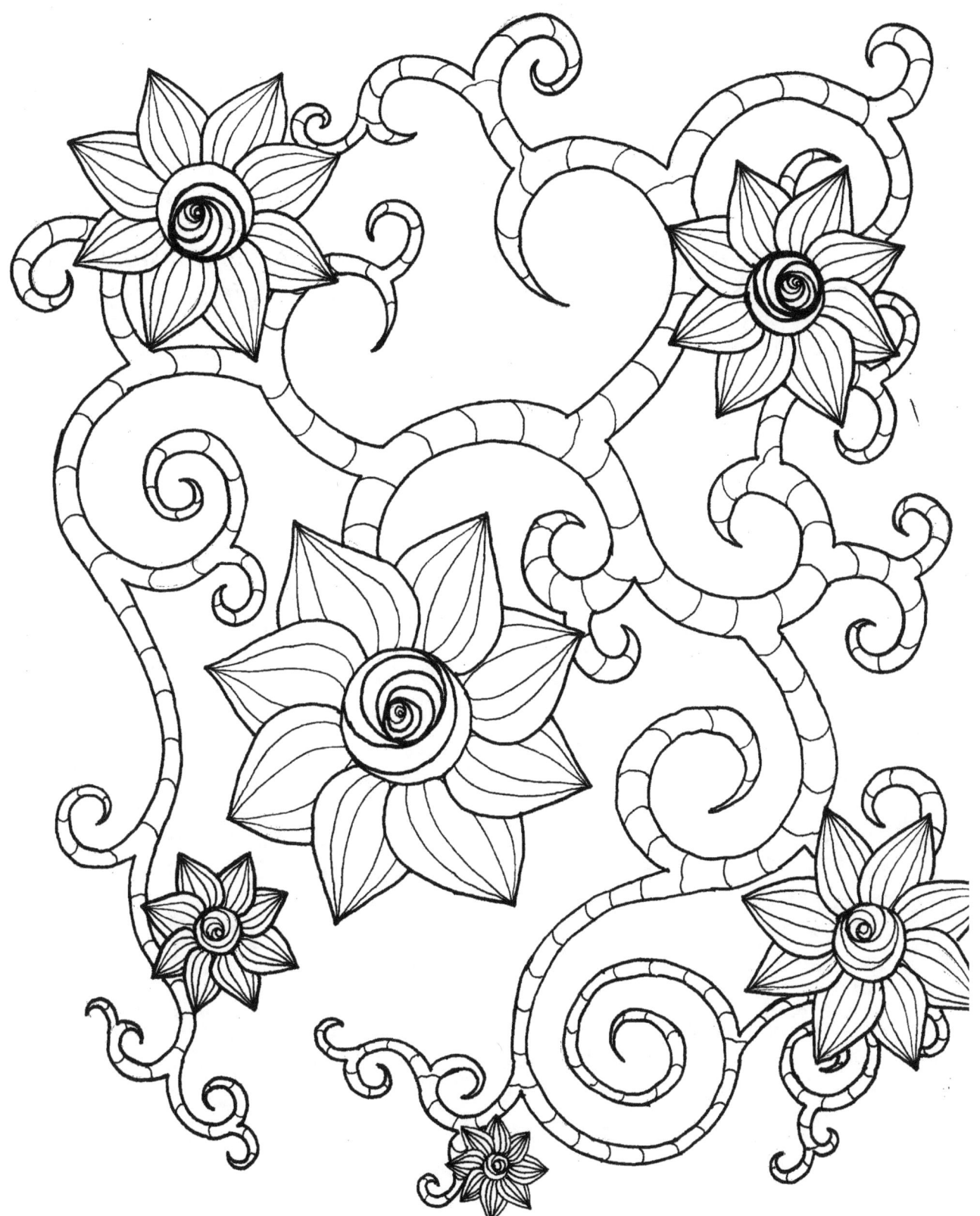

It would be great to have someone that take out every obstacle that gets in our way. Someone that can't be stopped from doing the right thing.

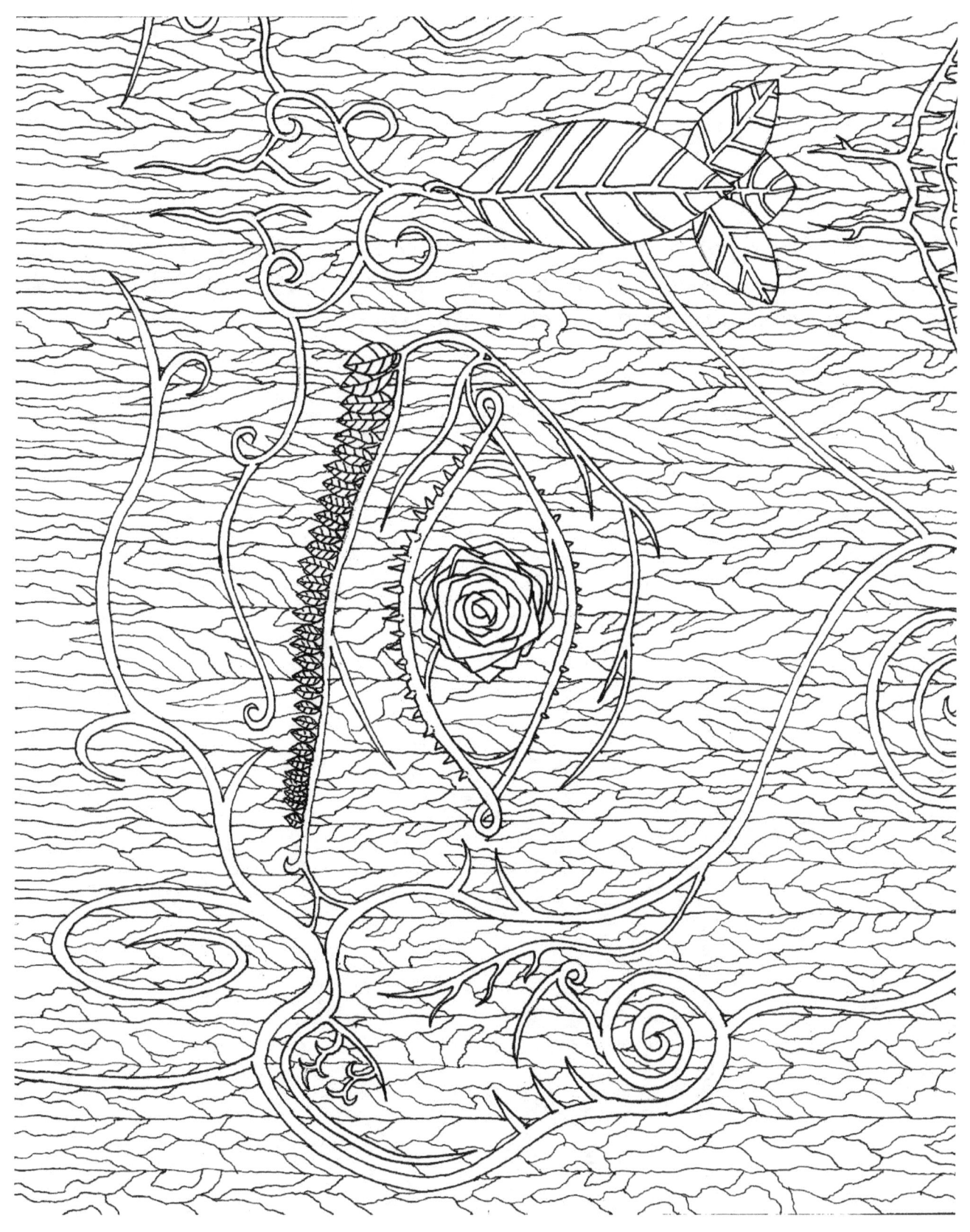

I challenge you to color this with all you got. Show us how you can create something beautiful and happy out of something that does not look happy. Get your passion and creativity to work.

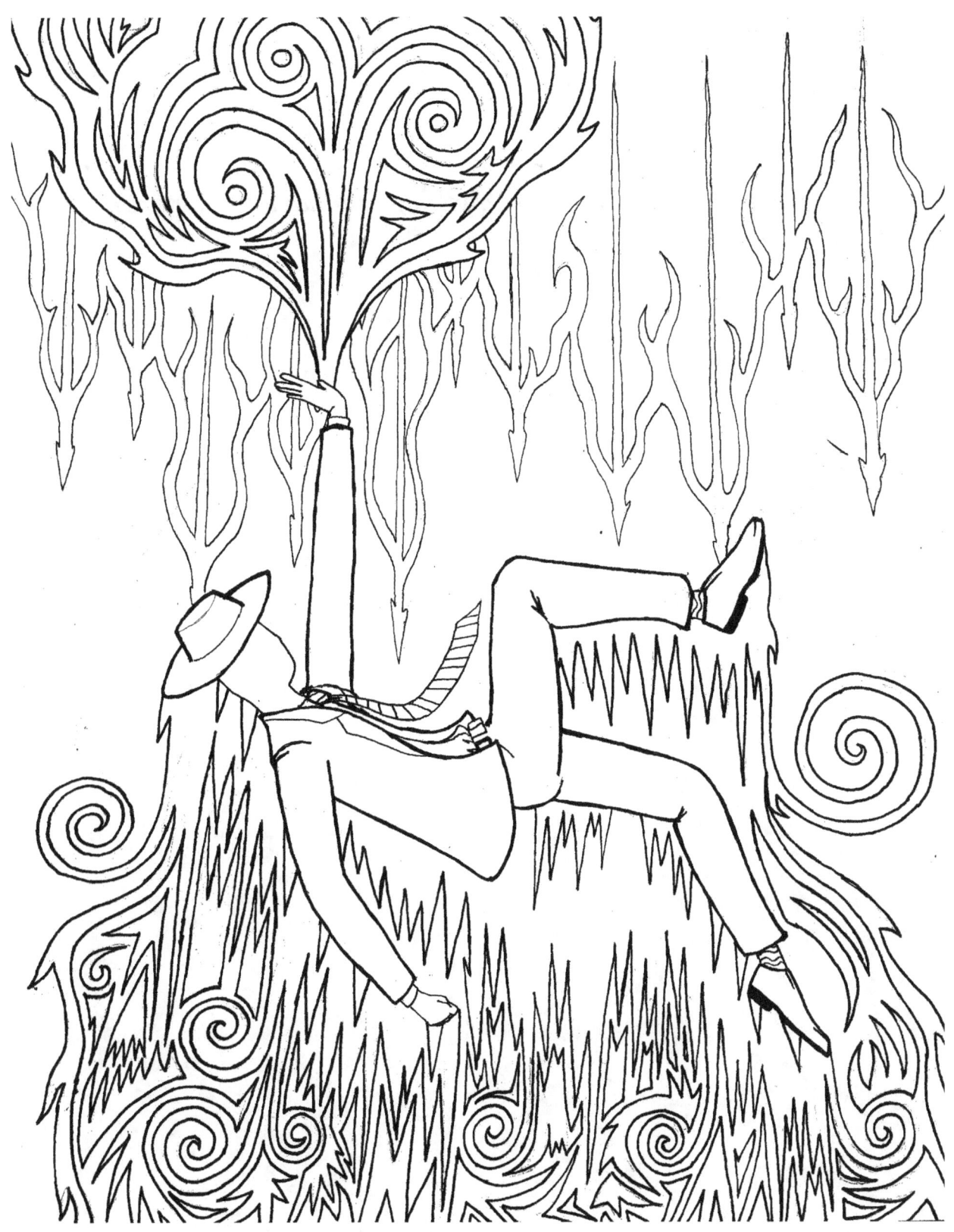

Monkeys are great. To color anything you have to be part monkey, and that is the truth.

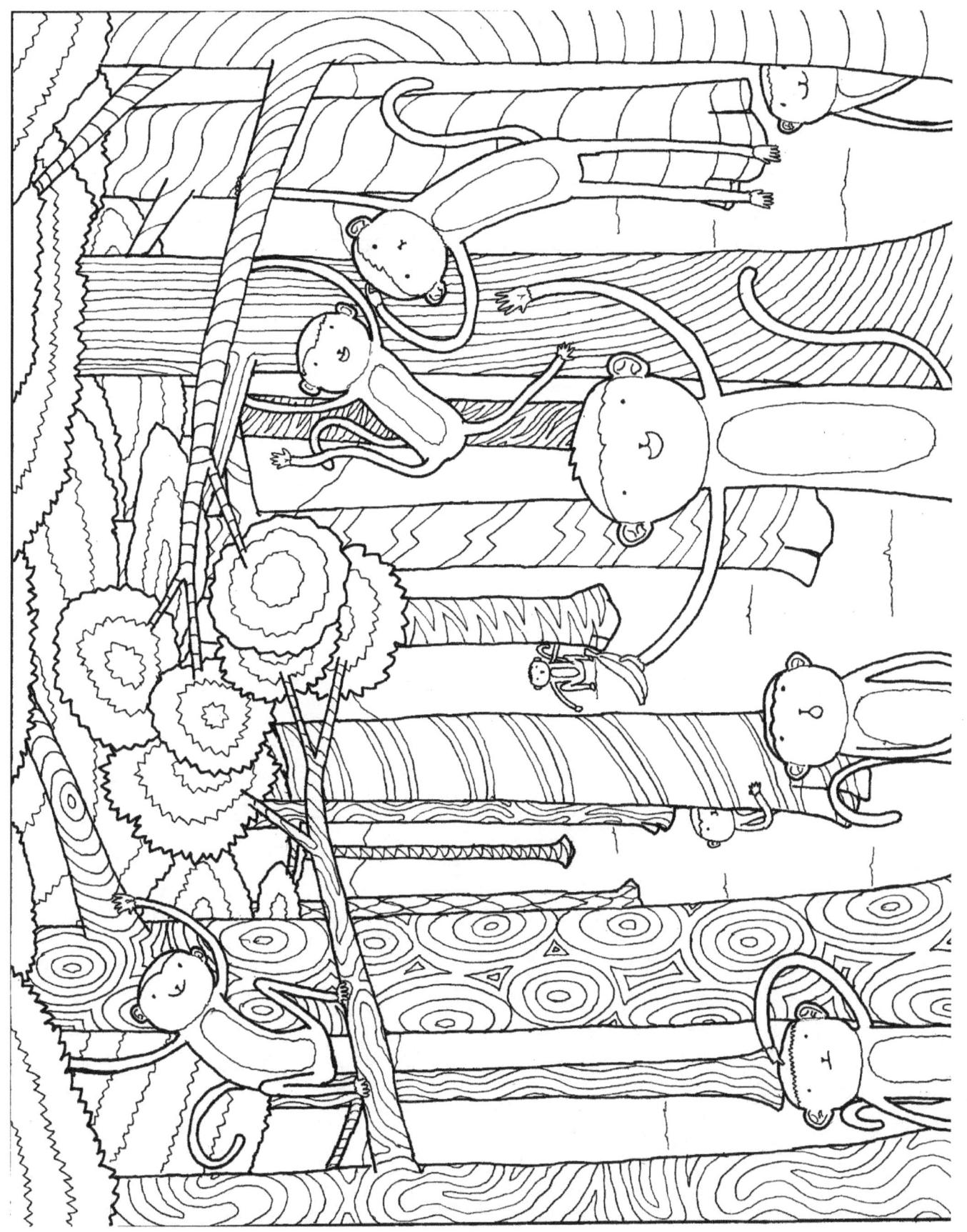

Don't you feel at peace when you see this tree?

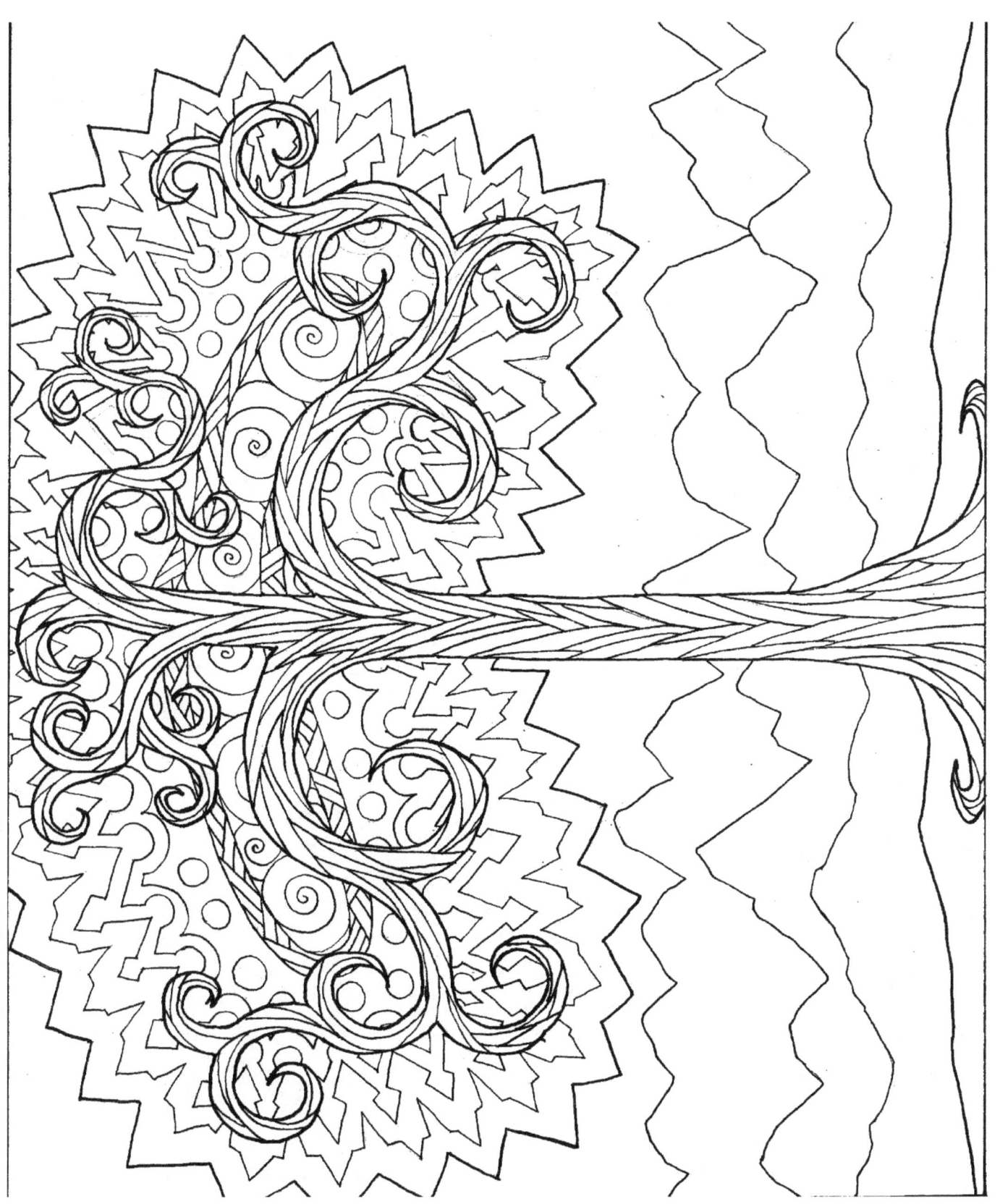

Everybody loves cats, everybody loves nature and everybody will love to color this cat.

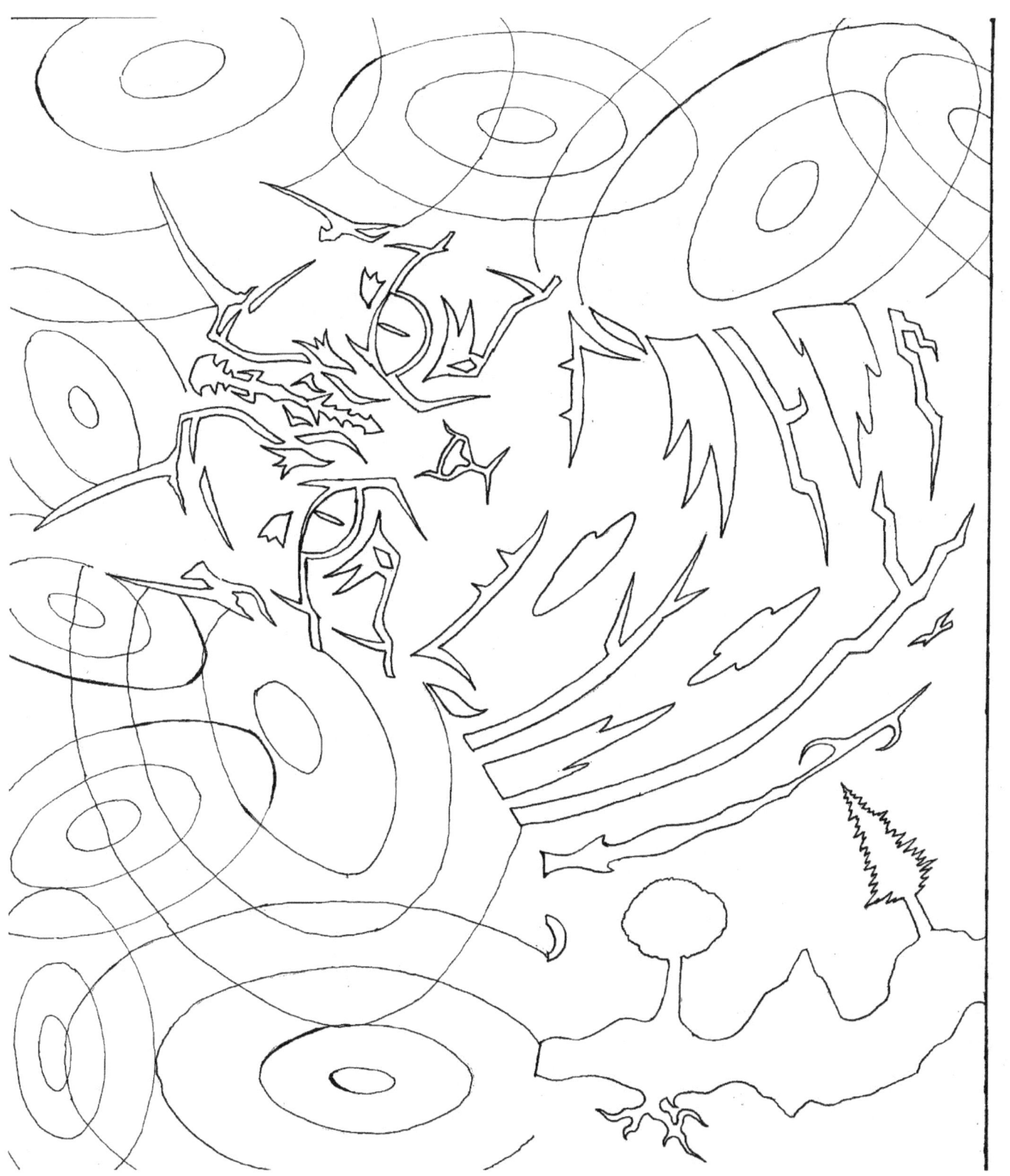

Here at Creativity Divinity we all love spirals. Nature gave us so many examples of spirals that we love. And humans have used their creativity to make variations spirals. Here is our homage for spirals.

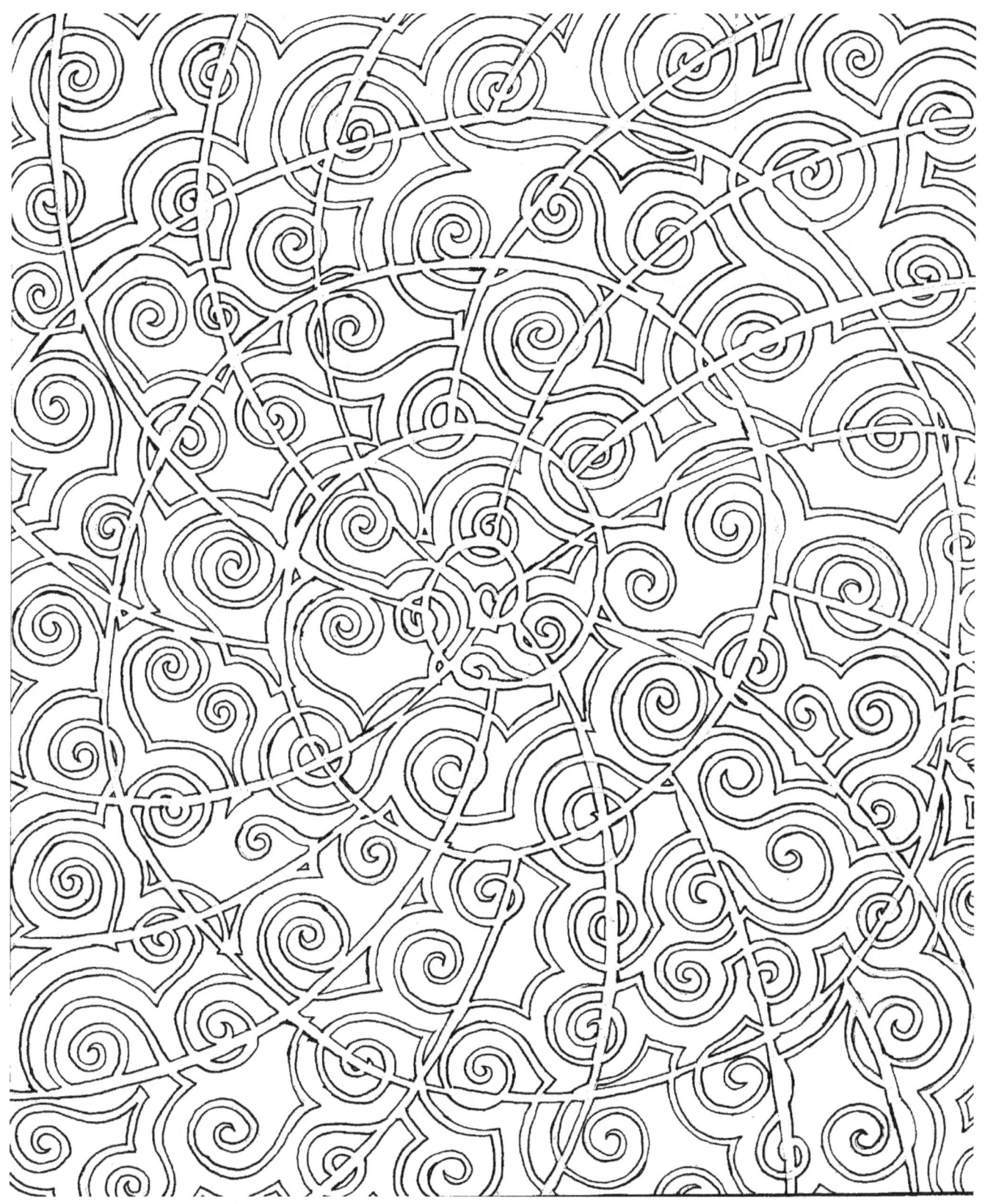

None of us are professional fashion designers, but we sure would love to see someone wearing this suit. In which color? For now, that's up to you.

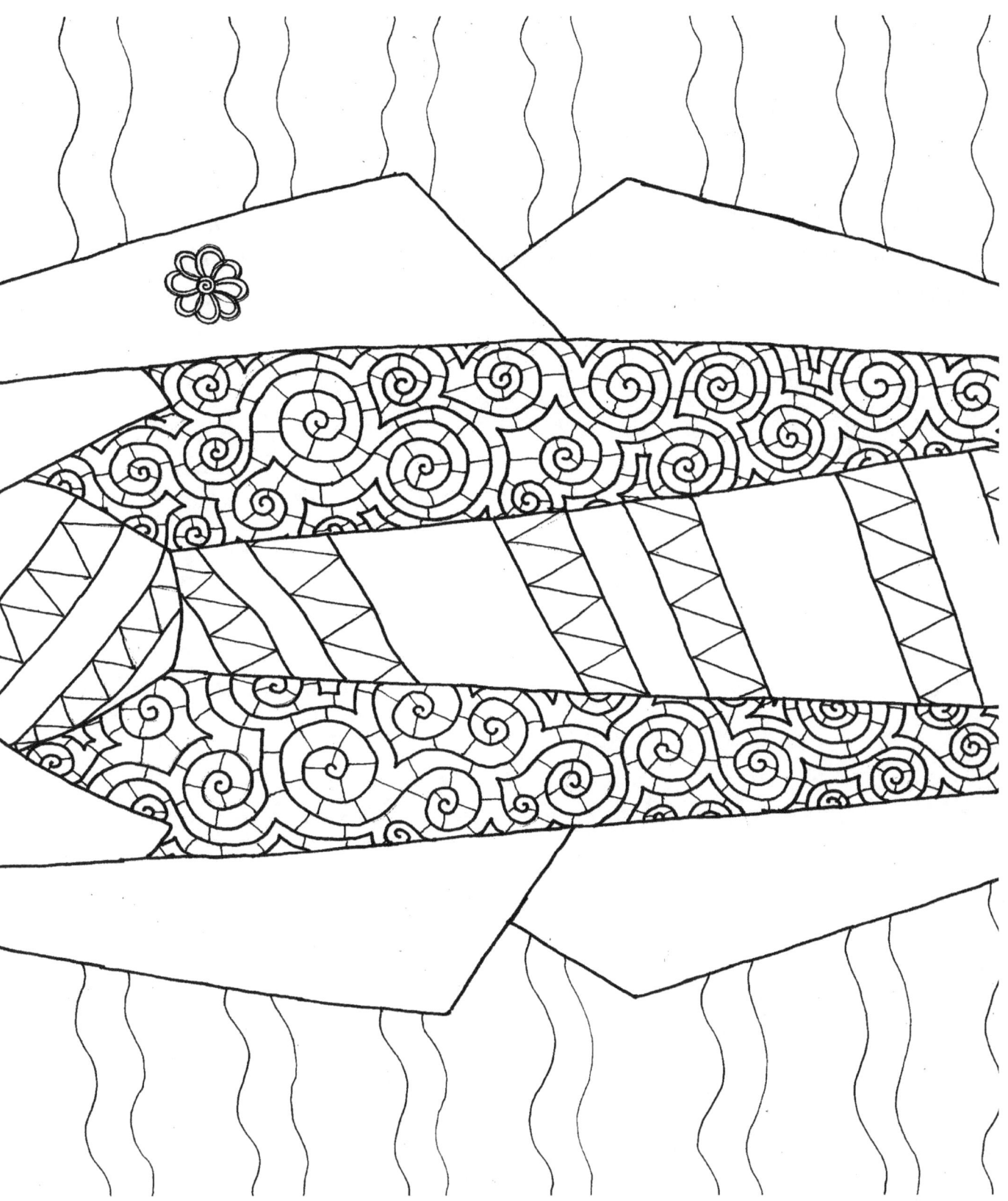

Leaves and cats are very different natural beauties. In our amazing imagination we can see those things together, and your amazing imagination will give them colors.

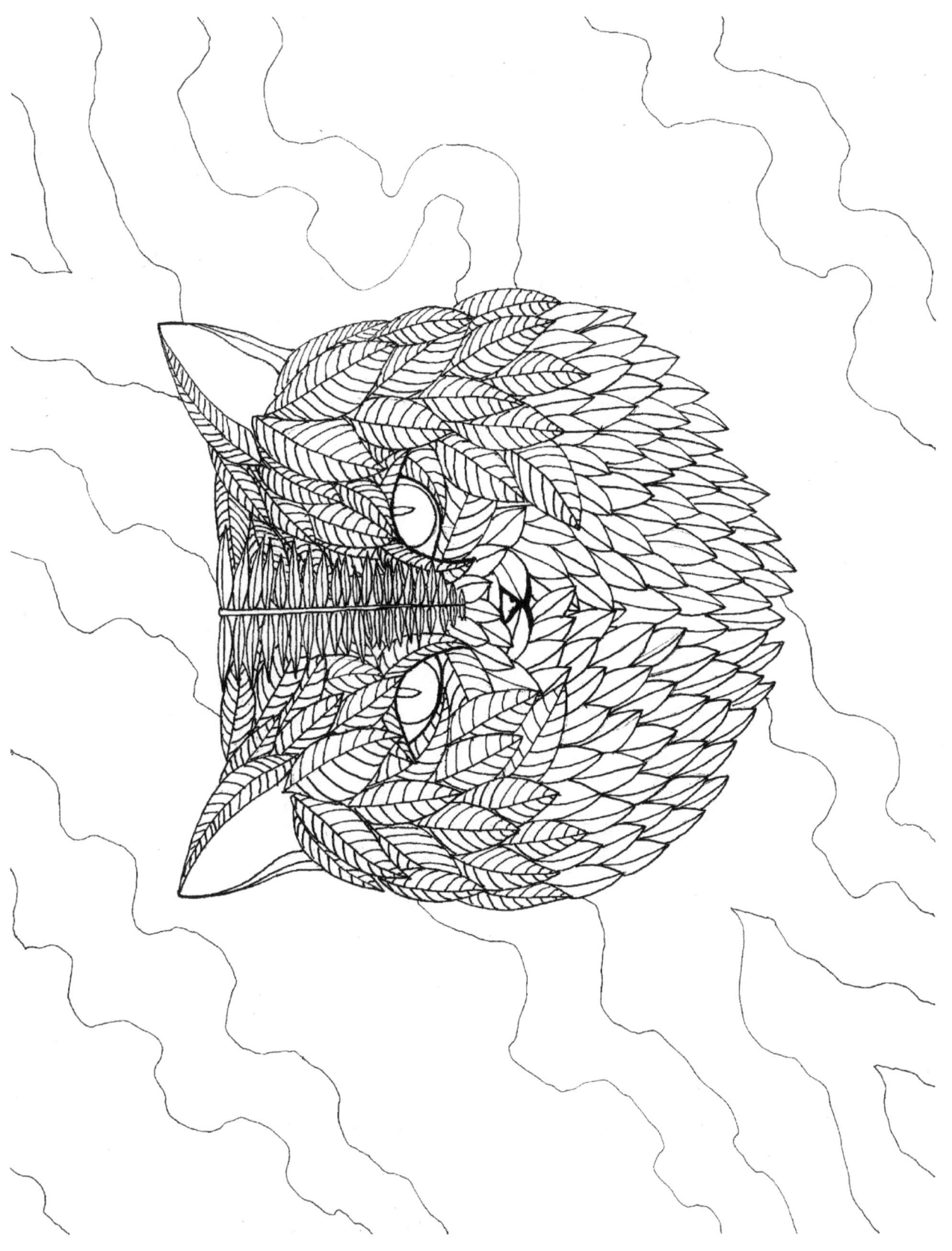

We all want to live in peace, it's in our nature. We are happier and we think clearer in a peaceful environment. That's why we want you to show how would this peaceful heart-shaped little town looks with colors.

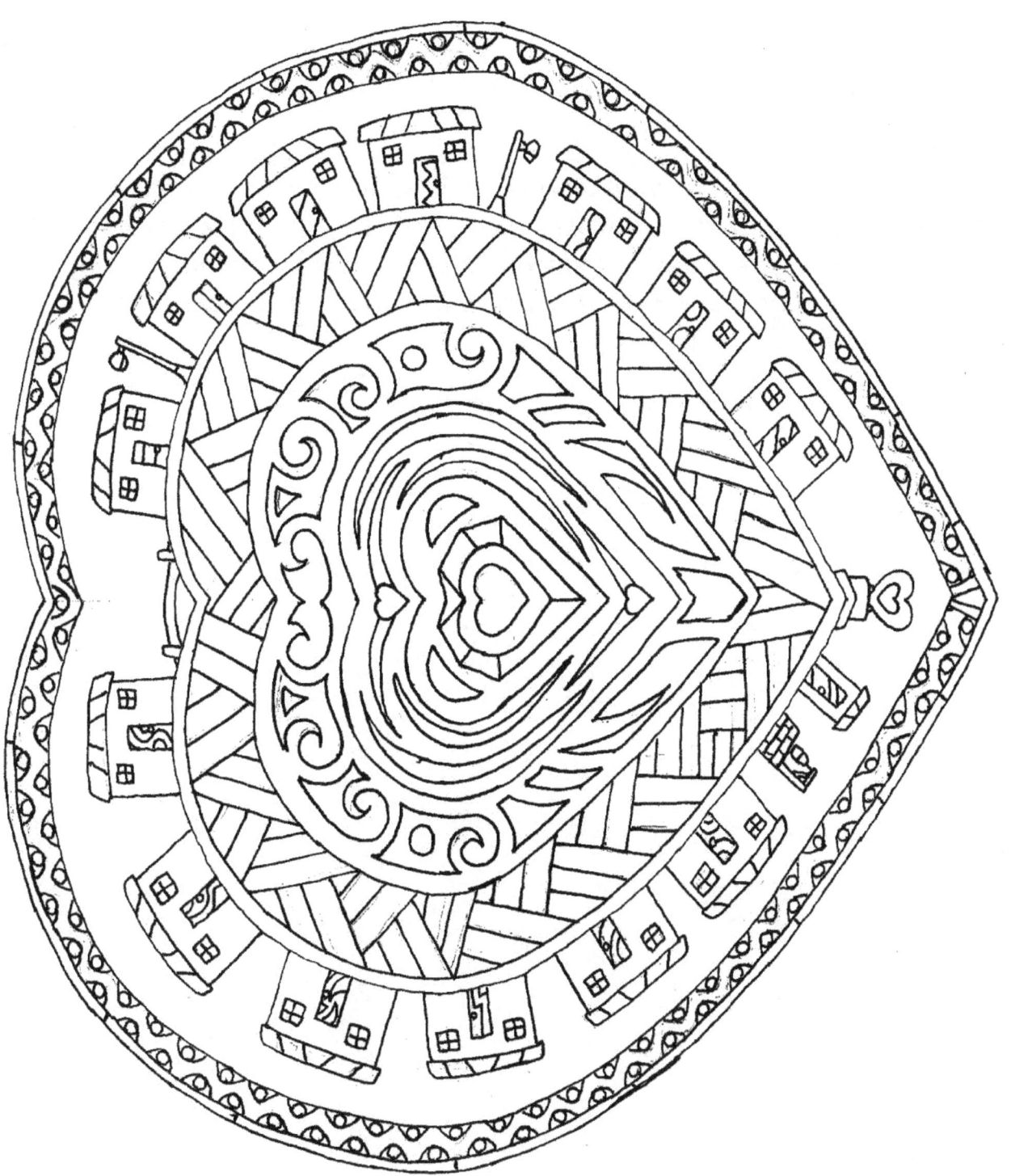

Sometimes we are happier just because we have someone by our side being our support. Those are the people we love. That person might be our partner, wife, husband, friend, brother, sister, anyone that by their actions prove that they are a big part in our lives. This one is for that special person. Show your love.

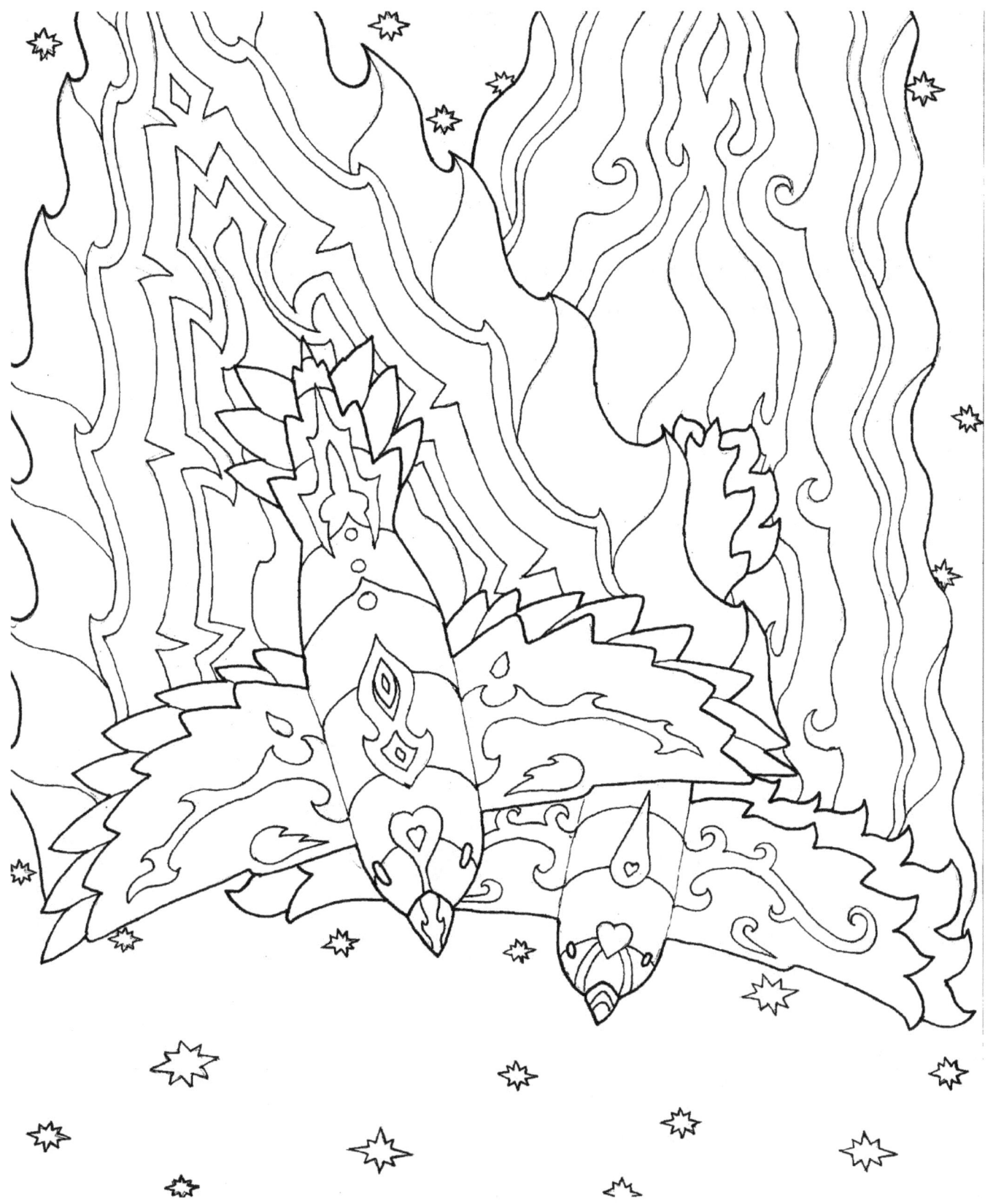

Like we told you before, everyone deserves to be happy, specially trees, after all they do live for us.

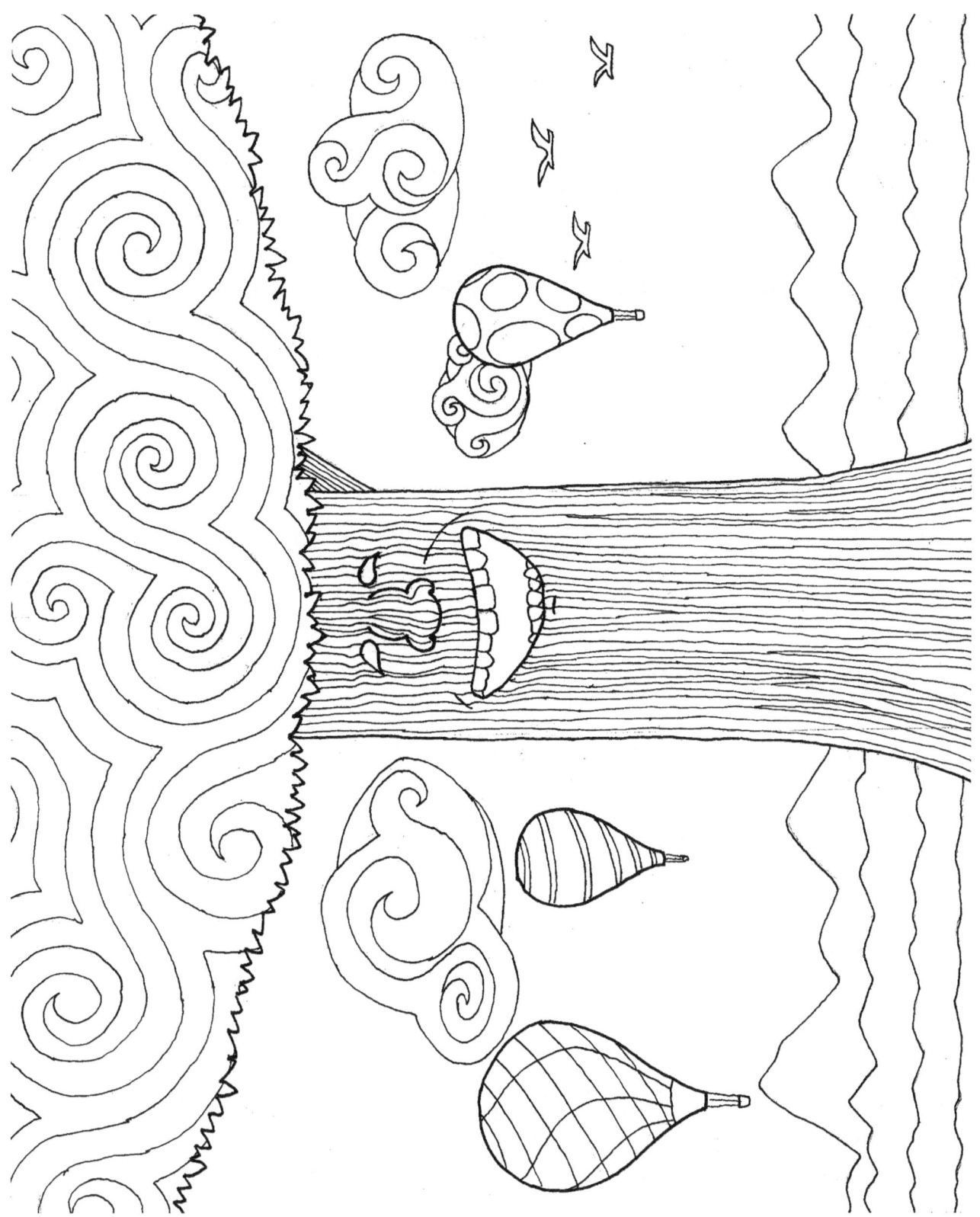

Every page that you have colored is a proof of how amazing our minds are. Not only you use it for every situation in your life and to keep you alive, you use it to entertain yourself. Our minds have such a creativity we can create things we have never seen before with all their details and beautiful colors. No machine can get close to that.

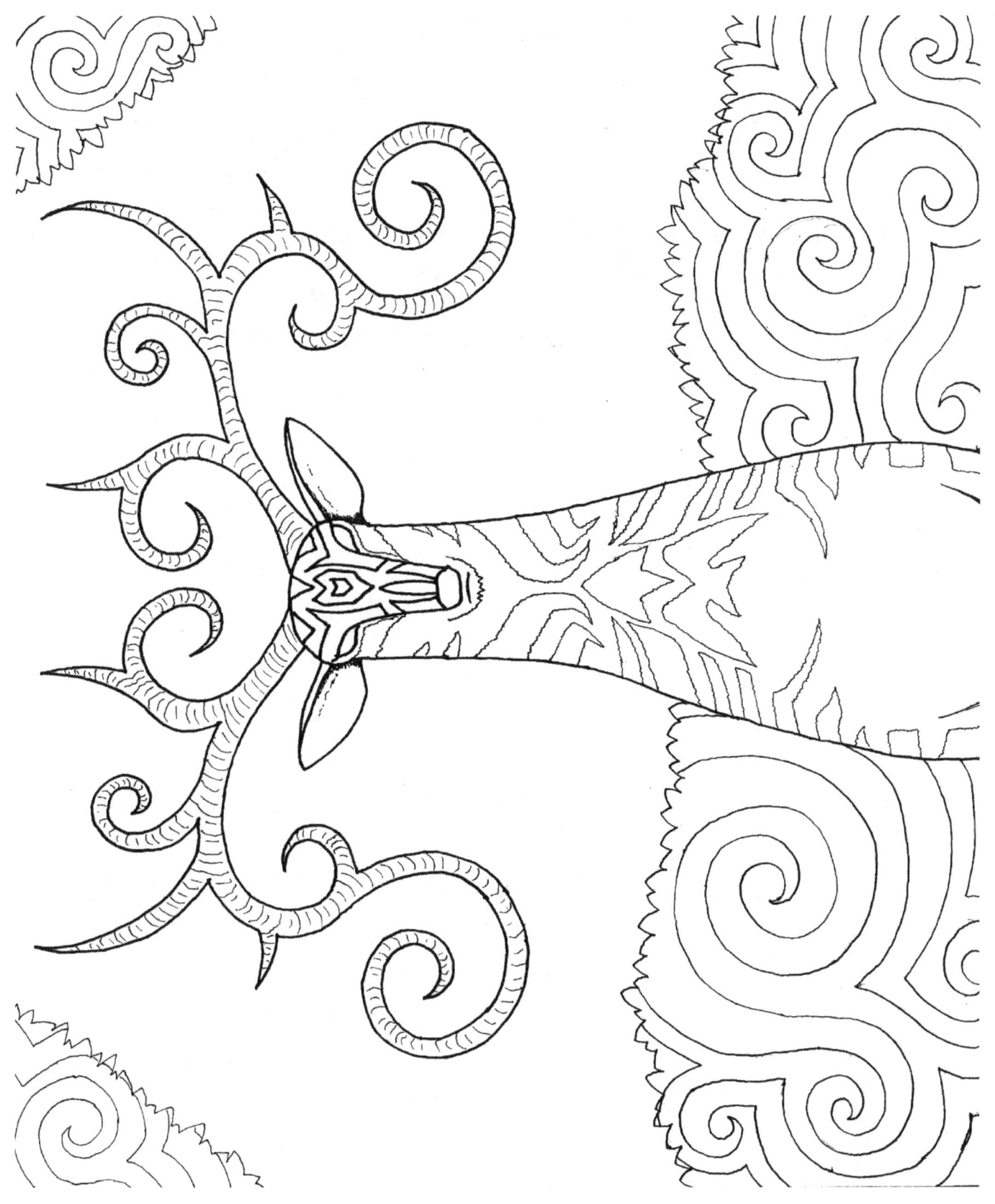

You feel relaxed, right? Do you feel your creativity working? I know it is, you're the best. Keep on coloring and show us what you got. We did half the job and you completed it, and we really want to see what your beautiful work. Post your work and tag us. And if you have any comments we will listen.

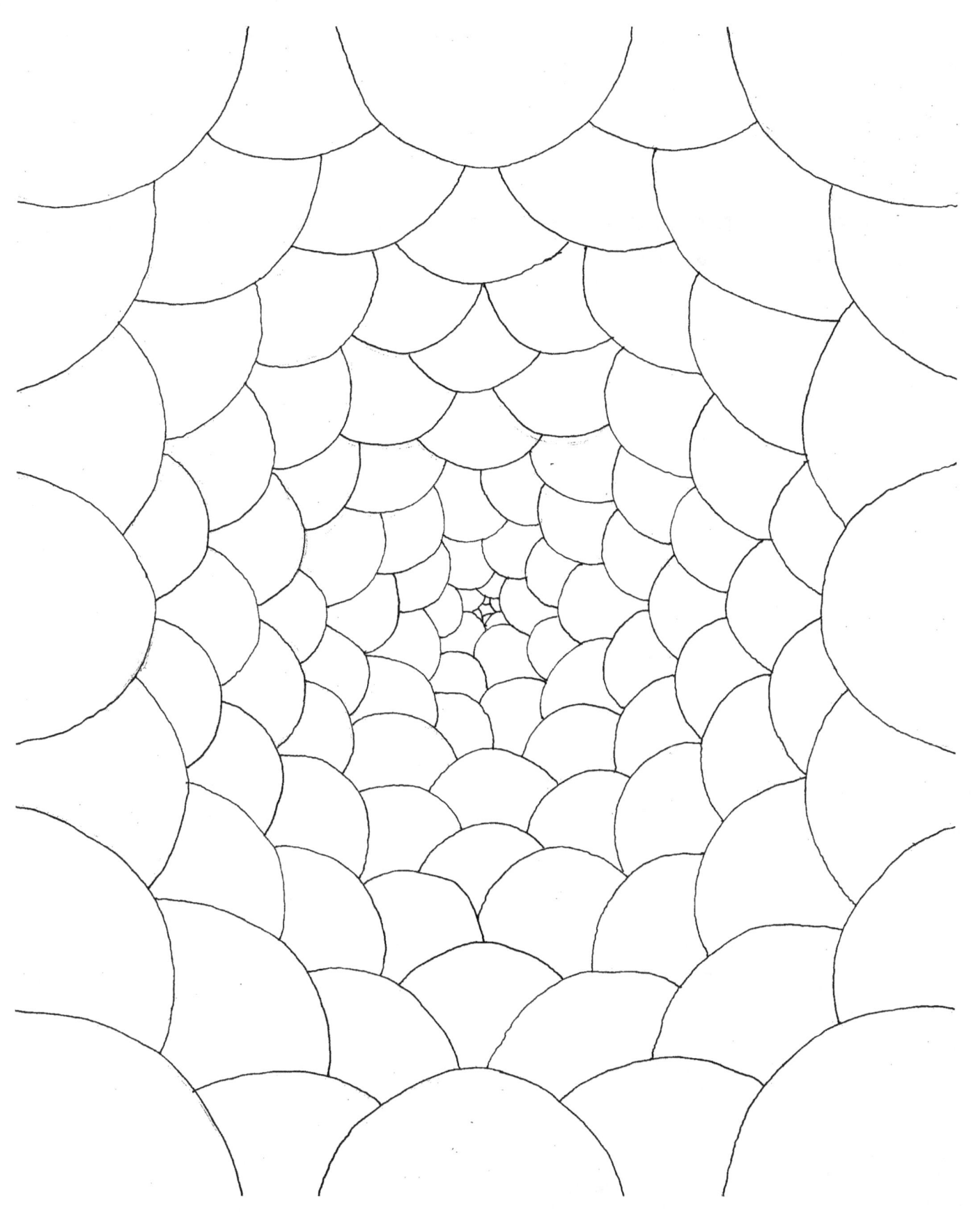

Post it on Instagram with the hashtag #creativitydivinityvol1 and tag us, @creativity_divinity.